Man WITH ADHD

Understanding the Intense Energy and Hyperfocus of ADHD in Men to Harness These Stealthy Strengths for Professional and Personal Growth and Unlocking the Hidden Benefits of ADHD

Dori Natasha Gentlekins

CONTENTS

Introduction 1

Chapter 1 3

Understanding ADHD in Adult Men

- Defining Adult ADHD

Chapter 2 12

The Science and Psychology of ADHD

- Neurobiology of ADHD
- Psychological Factors
- Behavioral Manifestations
- Addressing Misconceptions

Chapter 3 20

Strategies for Managing Symptoms

- Conventional Treatments
- Holistic Approaches
- Organizational Strategies and Time Management
- Exploring Alternative Therapies

Chapter 4 29
Professional Life and ADHD
Workplace Challenges
Leveraging ADHD Strengths
Legal Status and Discrimination Provisions
Networking and Support

Chapter 5 36
Relationships, Social Skills, and Emotional Regulation
Effective Communication
Social Interaction Strategies
Relationship Maintenance
Self-Esteem and Confidence
Conflict Resolution

Chapter 6 45
Harnessing ADHD for Personal Growth
Hyperfocus as a Strength
Risk Management and Decision Making
Creative and Strategic Thinking
Personal Goals and Motivation
Inspirational Success Stories

Chapter 7 52
Building a Sustainable Support System
Identifying Allies
Professional Help
Community Resources
Family Dynamics

Conclusion 59
Thank You 60
References 61

INTRODUCTION

Attention Deficit Hyperactivity Disorder (ADHD) is seen as a young child's problem. But for a huge number of adult males, these difficulties continue throughout their life. This book is the ultimate clear and complete guide to ADHD, which can be applied within the context of contemporary masculinity.

Unfortunately, the symptoms of the ADHD of adult men are often misjudged or they are simply ignored. Fast pacing, absent-mindedness and inability to concentrate on one task for a prolonged time are some behaviors related to ADHD, which can hinder both professional and personal aspects of your life. Another emotional experience noted is the emotional dysregulation in men in which they are unable to control their emotions, leading to emotional overwhelm.

While ADHD shows itself differently in different aspects of the population, the similarities and differences in how it manifests in men and women are notable. They may display more active behaviors that include physical aggression, lack of attention and hyperactivity. If untreated and undiagnosed, ADHD may grow to more complex difficulties in the future.

This book "de-mystifies" and makes the condition understandable and explains the science behind the effects of ADHD on the brain, in addition to providing consolidated multi-modal methodologies for managing its symptoms. Such a guide for men whether to accompany a formal diagnosis or personal understanding of themselves, irrespective of the reason, this guide will propel men with ADHD into understanding, accepting, and overcoming this condition.

Chapter 1

ADHD continues to be a neurodevelopmental disorder even in adulthood, significantly affecting adult males. Although ADHD is a prevalent problem for children, it can also stay with you when you become an adult. This can create some specific difficulties, ones which are often ignored or aren't understood by many.

The primary focus of this chapter is on the definition and diagnostic yardsticks of ADHD among men, with particular emphasis on its prevalence among this group of the population. Different masks can help conceal ADHD characteristics, for instance, cultural or social factors, those who suppress these behaviors, and stigma. Furthermore, we are going to go into how ADHD affects the world of emotional regulation, gender differences, and the significance of early identification.

Defining Adult ADHD

refers to the unique indicator of continued evidence of inattention, hyperactivity, and impulsivity, which together hinders in the process of regular tasks in any setting. Although commonly linked with childhood, these can also affect adults, making problem solving that mostly affects men quite a troubling experience, mainly due to ignorance.

Symptoms and diagnostic criteria

The symptoms and diagnostic criteria of ADHD, according to DSM-5, include the following symptoms:

1. **Inattention:**

- Difficulty in staying focused
- Easily distracted
- Forgetful
- Disorganized

For example: A 35-year-old engineer, John, feels his position is threatened by his inability to keep his attention in meetings. This results in him missing out on important details, leading to costly errors in his projects.

1. **Hyperactivity:**

- Restlessness
- Inability to remain still
- Excessive talking

For Example: Despite being in his 40s, Mike finds himself constantly fidgeting, tapping his feet, and interrupting others during conversations, which has strained his professional relationships.

1. **Impulsivity:**

- Acting hastily without considering consequences
- Interrupting others
- Difficulty waiting their turn

For Example: At 28, Alex frequently makes impulsive decisions, such as quitting jobs without a backup plan or spending excessively, leading to financial instability and regret.

In order to get diagnosed with ADHD, the patient must meet at least a few criteria specified in the DSM-5, the diagnostic guide. The standards comprise evidence as having symptoms earlier than age 12 and considerable deterioration in various places, including the workplace, relationships, and social setting.

Prevalence in adult men

The Centers for Disease Control and Prevention (CDC) cites that men make up from 4% to 8% of the overall population who suffer from ADHD in adulthood. Boys are three times more diagnosed than girls. Evidently, a significant number of cases that go undetected occur because of multiple issues. A 2021 study published in the

Journal of Attention Disorders by Liu et al. titled "Surge in Adult ADHD Diagnoses and Stimulant Prescriptions During the COVID-19 Pandemic in the US" illustrates the rise of ADHD in adults.

Unrecognized ADHD: Why It Happens

ADHD may be recognized in children, but it is often unrecognized in adults, especially in men. Several factors contribute to this phenomenon.

- **Social and Cultural Factors**

Societal expectations, gender roles, hours of service, and norms can influence people's perception and recognition of ADHD in adult men. Due to traditional male stereotypical ideologies, which utilize the downing of emotions and dependency on themselves solely, men might not open up about themselves or reach out for help. A case in point would be that of Mark, a successful businessman who had been dealing with disorganization and impulsivity for years, but he was worried that seeking help for ADHD would be referred to as a cowardly move in his industry, which is composed mainly of men.

- **Masking Behaviors**

Those without diagnosed ADHD as adults may have developed lively coping mechanisms and compensatory strategies to conceal symptoms; hence, the identification of the present condition may be harder in the first place. Such conduct often comprises over-fixating, self-medication, or modifying routines to be more routine-oriented. Kyle, a forty-two-year-old software developer, knew how to harness his ability to become deeply focused on his work; this featured his ability to focus hard for long periods of time. But he was fooling himself by just ignoring his ADHD struggle subconsciously, causing restlessness and emotional unbalance.

- **Stigma and Misconceptions**

ADHD usually appears in childhood and is often considered as a condition that should fade away over time. The misperception that only children and women are prone to mental health problems, along with the stigmatization of mental health conditions, can make adult men unwilling to seek proper treatment and diagnosis.

Emotional Dysregulation: The Hidden Impact

The hallmark symptoms of distress in adult men with ADHD include inattention, hyperactivity, and impulsivity, with emotional disturbance being the less explicitly known but very serious aspect of the condition. This emotional dysregulation can manifest in various ways:

- **Anger and Frustration**

Adult men who are hyperactive-impulsive by nature often get angry, frustrated, and overwhelmed with these feelings more emotionally and excessively than they are normally prescribed in accordance with their nature. Historically, speaking out came with baggage, which affected relations with friends and colleagues. Therefore, the problems go on and on. Take, for example, Dave, aged 38, who used to regularly become impulsive in anger and rage at close associates and clients about petty issues, which cost him very important accounts and harmed his reputation.

- **Impulsivity and risk-taking**

ADHD's impulsiveness can be exhibited in high-risk behaviors, such as drug abuse, driving without caution, or improper decision-making, which may have very adverse short- and long-term ramifications. At this point, Ryan was only 29 years old. He had failed two marriages, and he had been fired twice from his jobs because of his reckless actions, heavy drinking, and gambling.

- **Rejection Sensitivity**

Many adults with ADHD are overly sensitive to any expressed rejection or criticism, which often causes their emotional state to suffer, as well as problems in their relationships with others. Upon completing a successful presentation at his company, the 42-year-old, who is a marketing executive, Tom, felt bombarded by a fog of self-doubt and anxiety after a single unpleasant comment from a colleague, which resulted in the situation where he did not perform his tasks properly for weeks.

ADHD And Gender Differences

While ADHD affects individuals of all genders, there are notable differences in how the condition presents and is perceived in men versus women.

- **Presentation in Men vs Women**

Studies highlighted that the signs of ADHD differed in males and females. When exploring gender differences in

ADHD, predominantly boys' externalizing behaviors, such as hyperactivity and impulsivity, whereas the internalizing symptoms of inattention and emotional dysregulation, are more common among girls.

For example male adults with ADHD became more likely to exhibit the traits of restlessness, impulsivity, and physical aggression. In the case of female adults with ADHD, they determined they're more vulnerable to inattention, anxiety etc

Challenges in Diagnosis and Treatment

In a stereotyped case of societal judgment and gender discrimination, ADHD in men can give rise to many kinds of gender discrimination. Alongside gender inequalities, professionals in the healthcare field can be prone to discrimination; this can cause under-recognition or inaccurate diagnoses of ADHD in men.

Itt was found that over 40% of the male adult population with ADHD had experienced indifferent attitudes or false perceptions from primary care medi he vcal workers, and only 25% of their female counterparts reported a similar occurrence.

Moreover studies like The Social Context of ADHD in Men and Boys: Stigma, Help-Seeking Behaviors, and Treatment Adherence" by Wilens et al. (2014) and Gender Differences in ADHD Across the Lifespan" by Biederman et al. (2010) published in American Journal of Psychiatry etc indicate that significantly fewer adult men with problems seek medical attention or compliance with treatment plans, probably due to fear of discrimination, feeling unmanly, or having difficulty asking for help in society.

Importance of Early Identification

Recognizing and addressing ADHD in grown adults is crucial for stopping long-term outcomes and getting rid of it

- **Preventing Long-term Consequences**

The symptoms associated with undiagnosed ADHD in adult men can manifest broadly to include fewer achievements in school or their professions, the creation of ti 66red relationships, dependence on substance abuse, and even a few more mental conditions like social anxiety and depression.

A study by Barkley, R. A., Murphy, K. R., & Fischer, M. (2008). ADHD in adults: What the science says. Guilford Press discovered that men who grew up with untreated ADHD were more likely to have trouble at work (redundancy), money troubles, and experience higher rates of divorce than their non-ADHD adult male contemporaries.

- **Accessing Support and Resources**

Adult ADHD is a continuous condition that could have a considerable effect on a person's sense of existence. Early detection and diagnosis can be a gateway to powerful treatments like medicines, cognitive-behavioral remedy, and different assisting interventions. Such as medication (stimulants like Ritalin, non-stimulants), cognitive-behavioral therapy, behavioral interventions, educational accommodations, occupational therapy, social skills training, coaching/mentoring, and assistive technologies.

In end, understanding ADHD in adults is important for addressing the specific demanding situations and limitations this populace faces. By raising recognition, dispelling misconceptions, and promoting early identification, adults with ADHD can get the support and resources they need to control their symptoms and lead enjoyable lives.

CHAPTER 2

ADHD is a neurodevelopmental disorder, and its cause is the complex interaction of biological, psychological, and environmental variables. Having a scientific recognition of the condition's cognitive and psychological components is crucial for gaining a holistic understanding of the problem and appropriately dealing with the challenges, especially in adult males.

We will study ADHD neurobiology. It covers the altered structure of the brain regions, disturbed dopamine regulation, and working memory problems. It delves into the psychological aspects of emotional trauma through understanding environmental risk factors, inherited predispositions, co-occurring disorders, and life course development. In addition, it outlays emotional side effects, namely impulses, hyperactivity, inattention, and anger. For that reason, it goes beyond the lies and dwells on the complexity of ADHD.

Neurobiology of ADHD

ADHD originates from intricate brain functions and, more specifically, from areas involved in its manifestation and from neurotransmitters that regulate functioning in these areas.

Brain Regions Impacted

Neuroscience shows that, in ADHD-affected people, the prefrontal cortex, basal ganglia, and cerebellum are challenged.

The (prefrontal cortex) performs executive functions like attention, novelty detection, and constructive impulses. Brain imaging research has revealed a structural and functional gap in the region of PFC (prefrontal cortex) in ADHD individuals who demonstrate lowered capability in managing tasks, making decisions, and regulating themselves.

The is the module that controls locomotive behavior and reward mechanisms. It also works in areas of lifelong learning. The performs certain cognitive functions related to attention, working memory, and many others. Connections are the vital concept here in ADHD; connections between the cerebellum and other nerve tissues result in inattentiveness and executive functioning issues.

Apart from motor control, the cerebellum can also be illustrated through its role in cognitive processes, which include attention, working memory, etc. Interruptions between the cerebellum and other brain areas that are connected have been found to be associated with the inattentive and executive dysfunctions in individuals affected by ADHD.

- **Dopamine Regulation and Reward Pathways**

The neurotransmitter , concerning motive, reward, and attention, has been mostly focused in comparison to the primary example of ADHD. People with ADHD may present an uneven dopamine level, which results in a loss of concentration, a relentless need for instant gratification, and unwise, reckless behavior.

One actual situation that can be considered is Alex, a 32-year-old graphic designer who has ADHD. On the contrary, Alex tends to postpone his classwork until the last minute, which makes it hard for him to meet the deadlines even though he does have a lot of creative potential in terms of design. It's his temperament and difficulties with setting aside things for later that bring him to the quick pleasures of video games and social media instead of fulfilling his responsibility to heed timely goals and deadlines.

- **Executive Functioning Deficits**

The term executive functions subsume a variety of cognitive events, such as decision-making, organization, working memory, and cognitive switching. The people who have this disorder may not excel in these functions, which will be a heavy blow in their daily lives.

Specifically, Mark, 45, who has the challenges of ADHD, which always leads to the wrong placement of important documents and him failing to organize his time properly, so there are cases of missed deadlines and rough relationships with his clients.

Psychological Factors

ADHD is neither a purely biological phenomenon nor a psychological disorder; the involvement of psychological factors in its manifestation and the consequent effects cannot be neglected.

- **Environmental Triggers and Genetic Predisposition**

Although ADHD is still not fully understood, it is probably a complex intersection between genetic and psychological aspects. An individual with a family history of ADHD may have a higher genetic predisposition to it, with the environment that they are in also playing a role in the condition's development, such as prenatal exposure to toxins or shock.

- **Co-occurring Conditions: Anxiety and Depression**

ADHD is frequently seen in patients who have a host of psychological problems, like anxiety and depression. These comorbidities, in fact, only lead to aggravated conditions that are already difficult to manage and individuals need help to come up with comprehensive treatment options.

In a case study conducted by the University of Toronto, a group of researchers concluded that adult men with

ADHD and panic and/or depression reported a higher degree of sad mood, impulsivity, and functional impairment than those with ADHD alone.

- **Developmental Trajectories**

ADHD is a basic feature of the brain, and thus it encompasses various manifestations and implications that are unique to each individual. Some of the of the oldest generations may fight a relapse of symptoms since they continue to live with the condition after they reach adulthood.

The Milwaukee Study - A longitudinal case-control study following children with ADHD into adulthood, led by researchers at the University of Massachusetts Medical School and Medical College of Wisconsin, with collaboration from UCLA. adult men with continuous ADHD symptoms reported a higher level of struggle in academic, professional, and relationship areas than their peers.

Behavioral Manifestations

It's a rather difficult challenge to identify the neurobiological and psychological aspects that play a fundamental role in ADHD. In the end, the individual will have to cope with these factors in their daily life.

- **Impulsivity And Hyperactivity**

Instantaneity and restlessness are the two symptoms of ADHD showcased in their classic form. The ADHD patients could exhibit such behaviors as reacting quickly before thinking through the consequences, struggling to sit in one place, and experiencing restlessness or any excessive physical movement.

A real-life situation involving Michael, 38, who holds a sales manager's position with ADHD, will also be considered. During conversations, Michael is usually restless, and he starts to tap his pen and interrupt others; thus, the other side feels disrespected and thus, it is disruptive.

- **Inattention And Executive Dysfunction**

Such symptoms as absentmindedness and problems with executive functions may be revealed in different circumstances, including an inability to focus, poor short-term memory, disorganization, and disordered management of time.

To illustrate, David, a twenty-eight-year-old software engineer who has ADHD, fails to stay on track during his coding sessions, as he keeps being blocked by social media or other distractions. It could mean David committing errors like missing deadlines, which would lead to resentment from both him and the team.

- **Emotional Dysregulation**

Earlier in this book, it was pointed out that emotional dysregulation is a big part of ADHD, sometimes even left unnoticed. People with ADHD can often have very strong feelings, such as anger or annoyance, and may have great difficulty deflecting such intense emotions appropriately.

A recent study by Reimherr et al. (2005). Emotional dysregulation in adult ADHD and response to atomoxetine.

Biological Psychiatry, 58(2), 125-131 found adult men with ADHD and emotional dysregulation have higher rates of conflict with other people, job insecurity, and substance abuse than the other men who do not have emotional dysregulation.

Addressing Misconceptions

While the message of ADHD being understood is growing, there are many misleading myths and misconceptions, especially regarding the manifestation of ADHD in adult males.

- **Dispelling Myths About ADHD**

A commonly spread misconception is that ADHD is a preschool and child disorder people should, with time, have outgrown. Nevertheless, the studies mentioned previously consistently report that ADHD can be lifelong, with many of the adults requiring some support in various aspects of functioning throughout their lives.

Meanwhile, one myth is that ADHD is solely based on hyperactive or disruptive behavior. Along with ADHD, a key can be hyperactivity; however, as mentioned, some people may just manifest the inattentive form of the disorder, which is usually either misunderstood or missed.

- **Understanding the Complexity**

ADHD is a multidimensional and multifaceted disorder, which implies there should be an integrative view shedding light on neurological, psychological, and environmental causes. The different experiences and manifestations of ADHD among adult men need to be acknowledged.

Myths should be dispelled, and the complex nature of ADHD should, therefore, be introduced so that stigma is reduced, people have easier access to competent support and resources, and, consequently, the lives of individuals with this condition improve.

In conclusion, ADHD is a complex multifactorial neurodevelopmental disorder that involves the passing back and forth of biological, psychological, and environmental factors. Consequently, by having the neurobiological underpinnings, psychosocial explanations, and behavioral reactions published in the brains of adult men with ADHD, we will gain a further understanding of what they are facing. Debunking lies and presenting complex cases of ADHD to people is a major factor that, among others, helps eliminate stigma, enables access to support, and improves the quality of life of those affected.

CHAPTER 3

It is not uncommon for ADHD in adult men to pose several hurdles that might affect the dimensions of their entire lives: work, relationships, and general well-being. And so, it calls for meaningful strategies and an overall comprehensive approach enable people with this condition to thrive.

This chapter describes widely adopted conventional and holistic methods and provides practical suggestions on getting organized, focusing, and using alternative therapies that give adult men with ADHD the power to change their lives.

Conventional Treatments

ADHD management remedies do not operate on a similar principle; common therapies often help to ease the symptoms and improve daily functions for many who suffer.

1. **Pharmacological Interventions**

Medication is, most of the time, the vital part of ADHD treatment of which the two most prescribed are stimulant medications and non-stimulants. Both of these work by blocking the reabsorption of specific neurotransmitters in the brain, like dopamine and norepinephrine, which leads to greater availability of these chemicals, thus the control of impulses and attention improves.

Here are Some specific examples:

Stimulant Medications:

- *Methylphenidate (Ritalin)*

Blocks the reuptake of dopamine and norepinephrine, increasing their availability.

- Amphetamines (Adderall) - Also increase dopamine and norepinephrine levels by promoting their release and blocking reuptake.

Non-Stimulant Medications:

- *Atomoxetine (Strattera)*

A selective norepinephrine reuptake inhibitor, increasing norepinephrine levels.

- Alpha-2 agonists like guanfacine (Intuniv) and clonidine - Help improve norepinephrine transmission

1. **Behavioral Therapy Approaches**

Cognitive-behavior therapy (CBT) ranks as one of the most implemented methods Safren, S. A., Otto, M. W., Sprich, S., Winett, C. L., Wilens, T. E., & Biederman, J.

(2005), particularly among ADHD children through which they get to understand their thinking patterns, which form the basis of their behavioral patterns. CBT allows people to learn coping mechanisms, optimize time management, and organize their activities. It also gives them a set of tools for emotional and impulse management.

Adult men with ADHD are characterized by excellent outcomes after they underwent CBT, as they noted improved executive functioning, emotional regulation, and overall quality of life.

1. **Cognitive-Behavioral Techniques**

Other cognitive-behavioral approaches, including mindfulness-based strategies, are worthy allies in the fight against ADHD symptoms because of their potent capabilities. They hone the only aspect of life that is wholly controllable: the present moment, where people have the power to switch off mind-wandering and cultivate self-regulating abilities through various techniques.

Holistic Approaches

Besides the main treatment options, there are many men who are victorious over ADHD with the strategy of a holistic approach, which implies mixing different approaches.

- **Nutrition And Lifestyle Modifications**

All dietary modifications and lifestyle measures can impact ADHD symptoms. Excluding processed food, giving up sugar and caffeine, and alternatively increasing the intake of whole foods rich in essential nutrients may help us improve our focus and attention.

- **Exercise And Physical Activity**

Physical activity done frequently can improve ADHD symptoms. In exercise, both dopamine, and norepinephrine levels in the brain are increased, which allows for enhanced levels of focus and concentration, in addition to lowering unexpressed energy levels and stress.

A study by Gapin, J.I., Labban, J.D., & Etnier, J.L. (2011). The effects of physical activity on attention deficit hyperactivity disorder symptoms: The evidence. Preventive Medicine, 52, S70-S74. reviewed male adults who had ADHD and were also involved in the regular exercise of aerobic activities, showing an improvement in executive function, attention, and emotional regulation compared to those who did not.

- **Mindfulness and Meditation Practices**

Mindfulness and mind-traveling techniques can be the most powerful resources for struggling with ADHD symptoms, being both the moment awareness creator and the reducer of mind-wandering and the enhancer of self-control. These skills aim for the mind to be concentrated on the current moment, not worrying about distractions or about past or future scenarios.

A study by Zylowska, L., Ackerman, D.L., Yang, M.H., et al. (2008). Mindfulness meditation training in adults and adolescents with ADHD. Journal of Attention Disorders, 11(6), 737-746 about adult men with ADHD who were undergoing a mindfulness-based stress reduction program. The participants confirmed they noticed a considerable improvement in their ability to handle the symptoms, control their feelings, and manage their stress and anxiety.

Organizational Strategies and Time Management

Among the important obstacles for adult men with ADHD is the difficulty in the areas of organization, time management, and task completion. Luckily, there are many interventions and techniques to get rid of these problems.

- **Tools and Apps for Planning**

In the digital age, there are plenty of apps and software tools available for humans with attention deficit hyperactivity disorder. These apps can be used to create schedules, set reminders, and prioritize numerous responsibilities by using apps like , , , and .

- **Establishing Routines and Structures**

Setting up regular routines and structures that contribute to the formation of predictability and health is a good thing for those with ADHD. This could imply establishing regular times of sleep and wake, as well as arranging meals at the same time and designating spaces for work or studies.

Representatively, a real example is Mark, a 44-year-old writer who has ADHD. Through setting a fixed hour for waking up each morning, doing exercises, and then spending different uninterrupted hours of the day on writing, Mark appreciated more focused and productive work.

- **Prioritization and Task Breakdowns**

People who have ADHD frequently have difficulties with task prioritization and segmenting the big items of work into smaller parts. Tactics such as the based on the level of importance and urgency, while task breakdowns make heavy projects feel like a piece of cake. Urgent and important tasks get tackled first, important but not urgent tasks get scheduled, less important but urgent tasks get delegated if possible, and unimportant, non-urgent activities get avoided. This is how it works.

- **Meditation and Attention Techniques**

Sustaining focus and concentration is a big problem that adult men with ADHD are likely to come across, which affects their work performance and success in different areas of life. Though this can be overcome through certain tactics and methods that can help you stay focused and disregard distractions.

- **Mindful Awareness Practices**

Mindfulness approaches employing focused breathing exercises and body scans could boost mindfulness among ADHD individuals, which will help to make them more aware of the present moment and less likely to wander off in their thoughts. Through the practice of keeping the mind fixed in the present moment, people acquire the skill to stay focused and reject any diverting stimuli.

- **Environmental Modifications**

The physical atmosphere largely influences an individual's attention. Measures like decluttering, lowering noise levels, and using earphones that block outside sounds and soft music can help create an environment that is suited to focused work.

- **Goal-setting Strategies**

Having particular and reachable goals can help human beings with ADHD avoid distraction. Techniques like (Specific, Measurable, Achievable, Relevant, and Time-certain) goal setting can provide structure and clarity on the way to help you stay on course and screen your progress in the direction of better health.

Exploring Alternative Therapies

While traditional treatments and everyday functional strategies are widely used for ADHD management, there is a possibility that some adult men can also benefit from looking into alternative therapies as supportive backup.

- **Neurofeedback and Brain Training**

Neurofeedback is a non-invasive technique that consists of monitoring mind interest and giving on-the-spot feedback to people who desire to manipulate their mind waves. It has a very good effect on control of impulses, and emotional regulation in humans with ADHD.

- **Herbal Supplements and Dietary Changes**

Although greater research must be achieved, a number of people with ADHD have reported benefits from ingesting precise natural supplements or implementing particular dietary adjustments. For instance, dietary supplements together with omega-3 fatty acids, zinc, and iron may be used to observe their impact on the signs and symptoms of attention deficit hyperactivity disorder. It is necessary to book a session with a healthcare professional while supplementing with any herbs or enhancing a particular food plan, because some herbs and supplements may interact with drugs or produce unwanted side effects.

- **Art And Expressive Therapies**

For ADHD individuals, engaging in artistic creativity through art, music, or dance gives a fulfilling outlet that helps with self-expression and self-regulation. Through these actions, the level of stress can be decreased, focus and attention can be improved, and social well-being can also be provided.

A study by Haywood, S., Dwyer, R., & Boscombe, N. (2016). Art therapy for ADHD: A systematic literature review. International Journal of Art Therapy, 21(2), 55-67 focused on adult men with ADHD who explored an art therapy program. The participants indicated they felt calm and alert as they engaged in the creative process and there was a reduction in the impulsivity and emotional regulation that they were experiencing.

However, it is important to consider the fact that although alternative therapies can be of certain help for people, they should not be considered as a replacement for the medical prescriptions given by healthcare professionals.

To manage ADHD in adult men, a holistic approach has to be applied, which involves conventional treatment strategies, holistic medications, organizational techniques, time management skills, and alternative therapies. Through exposition and discovery of the most appropriate approaches for themselves, adult men with ADHD can address their symptoms and guide their way toward fulfilling and satisfying lives.

CHAPTER 4

The professional sphere can be a complex landscape to navigate for adult men with ADHD. While their condition may present certain obstacles in the workplace, it also unlocks a wealth of unique strengths and capabilities that can be invaluable assets in their careers. This chapter includes complaints about workplace challenges but also the individual's abilities and legal rights about helpful accommodations for those with ADHD. Furthermore, it asserts the values of networking with colleagues with whom you may share your ideas and advance professionally.

Workplace Challenges

Although ADHD may provide distinct abilities and outlooks that can benefit the productive environment, it can also generate several obstacles that can influence organizational performance and development.

- **Executive Functioning Demands**

Numerous jobs require a high level of executive function skills, among which are planning, organizing, time management, and task prioritization. People with ADHD encounter these types of challenges; thus, they experience a hard time with distributing time, tracking deadlines, and managing the demand from different sources.

- **Time Management Struggles**

Those with ADHD have certain problems with time management. This is expressed in constant delay, procrastination, and failure to complete tasks on time. This not only endangers the individual but also the team's structure and the project execution plan as well.

- **Communication and Interpersonal Skills**

Communication and interpersonal skills are also affected by ADHD; these abilities are fundamental in any workplace scenario. People with ADHD aspire to be treated with respect but may find it hard to listen, interrupt, and to control their emotions during meetings or conversations.

It was found that adult men with ADHD face the dilemma of sustaining positive working relationships due to miscommunications, impulsive answers, and an inability to deal with their stressful emotions during discussion. (Barkley, R.A. (2015). Emotional dysregulation is a core component of ADHD. In R.A. Barkley (Ed.), Attention-Deficit Hyperactivity Disorder: A Handbook for Diagnosis and Treatment (4th ed., pp. 81-115). New York: Guilford Press.)

Leveraging ADHD Strengths

Although the challenges of ADHD on the labor market are significant, the disorder may also bring certain specific talents and skills to the workplace, which can eventually result in meaningful and rewarding professional careers.

- **Creativity and Innovation**

A significant portion of those diagnosed with ADHD may be gifted with exceptional creativity and innovative mental power. They can use their imagination to outrun ordinary thinking and could easily become useful in jobs that are very creative and require advanced problem solving.

- **Problem-Solving Abilities**

People with ADHD frequently demonstrate their skillfulness in working with patterns, making links, and giving answers to complicated issues. In work situations that are very dynamic, those who think critically and can readily respond to the shifts are worth their salt.

- **Hyper Focus in Productivity**

Although ADHD can make it hard to maintain an emphasis on routine jobs that are unenticing, one of the outstanding abilities of this condition is the ability to hyper-focus on tasks that the person finds most captivating. This strong concentration can produce brief spates of productivity and shining work should a situation be handled effectively.

Legal Status and Discrimination Provisions

Employed adult men are provided with work-related legal rights and are eligible for reasonable work-accommodating measures to facilitate their performance and success.

- **ADA Protections and Workplace Rights**

As in keeping with the (civil rights law that prohibits discrimination against individuals with disabilities in all areas of public life, including jobs, schools, transportation, and all public and private places that are open to the general public.), it is illegal for employers to discriminate towards processing applicants with ADHD and other disabilities. According to the ADA, employers must offer reasonable accommodations to candidates with disabilities who meet all qualifications for the job unless it would make such an adjustment for a company to be considered "unreasonably exhausting." (The Americans with Disabilities Act of 1990 (ADA) was signed into law on July 26, 1990 by President George H.W. Bush.)

- **Requesting Reasonable Accommodations**

Those who struggle with ADHD are seeking reasonable adjustments that aim to alleviate the effects of this condition. Examples of accommodations can include:

1. Having a flexible schedule or working from home.

2. Using noise-canceling ear plugs or having a quiet place to work, such as a library.

3. Efficiency can be improved by the use of organizational apps and software.

4. The exhaustion of deadlines or adjustment of the workload.

5. Indicating what has to be done or what response is expected in the text.

It seems appropriate for a person to cooperate with the employer and HR team in order to find out the actual accommodations specific to their needs and the job's requirements.

- **Disclosing ADHD to Employers**

To tell the management of a company about an ADHD diagnosis or when to do this is a decision that has to be thought over and analyzed. Whereas a positive aspect lies in such disclosure as the availability of accommodations and supports, there may be fears about stigma and discrimination.

Most adult men with ADHD admitted that sharing their condition with their employers resulted in a positive experience. The increased support and understanding by their employer, which is based on their knowledge about ADHD, had a positive impact on both their job performance and satisfaction.

Networking and Support

It is not a rarity that establishing a good professional network and support group can be very beneficial for adult men with ADHD, where men can gain mentorship, share resources, and have a sense of community.

- **Building Professional Relationships**

By creating a web of positive connections with colleagues, mentors, and industry experts, you can uncover an infinite source of new chances, get informed and supportive advice, and find a group of like-minded people who help you face professional problems.

- **Mentorship Opportunities**

Mentors can impart both theoretical and practical knowledge, teach problem-solving techniques, and be a source of mental support. This goes a long way toward helping and guiding individuals' professional journeys.

Goldstein, S. (2005). Coaching as a treatment for ADHD. ADHD Report, 13(5), 6-8. conducted a study with male ADHD adults who had mentors, and they rated their job satisfaction higher, gained confidence, and had better career advancement compared to those without a mentor.

- **Joining ADHD-specific groups and communities**

Communicating with people who have ADHD can give you feelings of unity, security, and acceptance. ADHD-tailored groups and online forums provide helpful opportunities for sharing useful resources, viable coping techniques, and personal stories. Consequently, an environment for successful professional career development and personal enrichment is formed.

To sum up, working with ADHD while at work involves several hardships, but it also makes it possible to capitalize on distinct strengths and achieve success through legal protections, arrangements, networking, and building a support group. Through recognizing their rights, eagerly promoting their needs, and valuing their own gifts, males with ADHD can excel in their preferred careers and attain their own professional goals.

CHAPTER 5

Restoring and improving communication skills, social interactions, and emotional regulation could be especially problematic for adult men with ADHD. Yet, after learning how to deal with such challenges, people know how to develop strategies and appropriate coping mechanisms to create fulfilling relationships and foster emotional balance.

This chapter provides the most useful methods of communication, social interaction techniques, means of relationship maintenance, strategies for building confidence and self-esteem, as well as healthy conflict resolution.

Effective Communication

In a personal or professional relationship, the foundation of all healthy communication is based on clarity and respect. People with ADHD can be especially helped by this skill in mastering effective communication. Interpersonal relationships become easier to manage.

- **Active Listening Techniques**

An important component of effective communication is active listening. It requires mentally devoting all attention to the speaker, recognizing their message, and giving a fitting response. Techniques include eye contact, avoiding interruptions, and summarizing the speaker's points can be very helpful in perfecting your active listening skills.

- **Assertiveness and Boundary Setting**

Assertiveness is the capability of advocating for one's needs, thoughts, and feelings in a direct and respectful manner while simultaneously inviting others' opinions. People with ADHD should learn to be assertive to avoid confusion, conflict, and develop friendships.

Adult men with ADHD who received assertiveness training showed increases in their skills and ability to set appropriate boundaries, effectively assert demands for their needs, and nurture positive relations.

- **Conflict Resolution Skills**

It is hard to avoid conflicts in relationships, but ADHD cases with emotional flare-ups and impulsivity can be aggravated by disagreements. Being able to implement conflict resolution skills, for example, active listening, empathy, and compromise, can give you more advantages in those situations.

Social Interaction Strategies

Social interactions can be hard for individuals with ADHD due to problems with decoding social cues, self-control of emotions, and managing their spontaneity. Through the creation of result-oriented approaches, adult men living with ADHD can explore such predicaments with a higher degree of self-esteem and, as a result, build deep-rooted relationships.

- **Reading Social Cues**

A good grasp of social cues and correctly interpreting them, like someone's body language, facial expression, and tone, is mandatory if we want to become successful socially. People with ADHD will most likely profit from learning the skill of attentive depiction and getting comments from good friends or relatives.

- **Navigating Group Settings**

Group environments usually create the risk that an ADHD individual can feel overwhelmed by the increased stimuli or social demands in such a setting. Tactics, which include coming early to jell with the environment and taking breaks as needed to recharge, will help in maneuvering challenges that may be brought about by group interactions.

According to a Antshel, K.M. & Olsten, T.F. (2014). Social skills training in integrated cognitive behavioral therapy for ADHD. Child and Adolescent Psychiatric Clinics, 23(4), 825-842., adults with ADHD enrolled in social skills training programs showed increased confidence and reduced anxiety when in groups, and this became evident after they learned discipline techniques for their attention and conversation management.

- **Overcoming Social Anxiety**

Several people with ADHD are more fearful and preservative in social situations, and, unfortunately, they avoid being in the presence of others and withdraw into solitude. CBTs, including challenging negative ideation, practicing relaxation methods designed for social anxiety disorder, and gradual exposure, may assist in making social anxiety less of a negative impact on someone's life, and that person may socialize safely and confidently.

Relationship Maintenance

In addition to the difficulties associated with all relationships, a great number of men with ADHD have to face special requirements for male-male connections and the nature of relationships between males and females. While this has the potential to negatively impact individuals' social lives, designing reliable techniques may make it possible to have clear and fun relationships with people you love.

- **Building Intimacy and Trust**

Unity and trust are the most valuable elements to be found in any good relationship. For individuals with ADHD, if intimacy should be fostered, it might entail special kinds of contact, which would be: Listening to and talking about everything that they feel and think, which takes place around their partner; certifying that communication is open and honest; and, finally, showing genuine interest.

Mature men with ADHD in therapy improved their emotional intimacy, communication, and relationship satisfaction as their knowledge of the strategies of building trust and emotional connections improved.

- **Handling Rejection and Criticism**

People with ADHD could be more vulnerable to feelings of rejection or criticism, as emotional dysregulation and a decrease in self-esteem could be among the reasons. Developing healthy coping strategies like cognitive reframing, self-compassion, and seeking support from others can help us deal with this.

- **Balancing Independence and Dependence**

Adhering to an equilibrium of autonomy and dependence in relationships is, in some ways, a difficult task with ADHD. Although independence is very important, getting support and establishing cooperation with loved ones when the situation is necessary is the key to making the relationships stronger and more secure.

Self-Esteem and Confidence

ADHD patients sometimes have low self-esteem and self-confidence as they face the societal stigma and the challenges that come with their condition. While this may involve learning to accept oneself and appreciating victories, adult men with ADHD will build good self-esteem and be successful in different situations.

- **Overcoming Shame and Guilt**

In fact, a good number of people experiencing ADHD have those feelings of guilt and shame because of their own failures or wrong perceptions of the condition in society. Negative self-talk can be overcome by challenging it, and people may find comfort and solace by sharing their struggles with others who also have ADHD, while educating themselves on the disorder can help promote a self-compassionate outlook.

It's confirmed that men with ADHD who were a part of a support group in which they have been encouraged to be accepting themselves suggested better shallowness and fewer feelings of shame and guilt.

- **Celebrating Achievements**

People with ADHD are usually biased towards reflecting equally on their struggles and strengths, discounting their strengths when they accomplish things. If you make a conscious effort to publicly recognize and celebrate even small accomplishments, then you will lift your self-esteem and secure a healthier self-image.

- **Cultivating Self-Compassion**

Compassion focused on oneself is about behaving towards oneself with a lot of kindness, understanding, and acceptance, especially in tough periods. When such people face more frequent setbacks and frustrations, self-compassion, which can help neutralize self-criticism and lift emotional wellbeing, is recommended.

The study by researchers at the University of California, Los Angeles (UCLA) confirmed that men with ADHD who were a part of a support group in which they have been encouraged to be accepting themselves suggested better shallowness and fewer feelings of shame and guilt.

intervention efficacy of self-compassion on an adult male population with ADHD. Many participants reported that they had reduced criticisms about themselves, had become much more accepting or self-assured, and experienced improvements in their general well-being as a result of learning to feel more compassion towards themselves through mindfulness meditation and shifting their focus from negative to positive.

Conflict Resolution

Appropriate conflict resolution is crucial for sustaining healthy relationships among people and envisioning their mental state. For ADHD patients with the tendency to develop high levels of impulsivity and heightened emotional reactivity of this type, the strategies help them when it comes to emotion management and communication, and when the need arises, they can seek professional help.

- **Managing Anger and Frustration**

Those affected by ADHD become quite emotional; for example, being irate or angry becomes more and more intense. Learning through tools like deep breathing, mindfulness, and cognitive reframing how to interfere with emotions in order to avoid reaching a point where a situation can escalate any further is also a good thing.

- **Negotiation and Compromise**

Negotiation falls within the category of optimal conflict resolution, while bargaining sees reaching a solution, particularly through compromise. Individuals diagnosed with ADHD who commonly struggle with impulsivity and emotional management might deal effectively with a conflict by having an open mind, paying full attention to the point of view of the person they are having a conflict with, and putting themselves in a best-paying situation.

- **Seeking Professional Help When Needed**

While we should all make efforts to develop personal strategies to resolve conflicts, situations may arise when one will need to seek the help of an expert, for example, a conflict that is recurring or where the parties are deeply entrenched. Couples counseling, family therapy, or individual counseling can be powerful tools used to help with interpersonal dynamics. They provide unique levels of support and guidance in this area.

Therefore, we can find that friendships, social and emotional skills can have different issues for adult men with ADHD. If people master communicative practices, socialization approaches, relationship maintenance methods, self-esteem, and confidence building, then they will have meaningful relationships and good emotional wellbeing. Equipped discreetly with the right tools and support, the adult male with ADHD can successfully manage his personal and career life experiences.

CHAPTER 6

ADHD brings along its own peculiar set of battles but can be the trail of the unconventional strengths that one can enhance through self-development. This chapter focuses especially on how the positive aspects of adult men's lives with ADHD may differ in how they approach success, nurture creativity, and enjoy both personal and professional fulfillment.

Hyperfocus as a Strength

One of the underrated benefits of ADHD is the ability to go into a hyper focused mode, which is a very potent cognitive resource when you know how to make use of it.

- **Channeling Intensity into Projects**

People with ADHD can be so overwhelmed when facing tasks and projects they enjoy; as a result, they might develop a strong sense of concentration and productivity.

Through clarifying what stirs their interest and putting it in line with their objectives, guys with ADHD can use their hyper-focus to do amazing things.

- **Setting Boundaries for Healthy Engagement**

Though hyper-focus might be the reason behind a task well done, it takes boundaries to ensure that you don't overshoot. Engaging in activities or projects repeatedly for a prolonged period unconsciously deprives the mind of rejuvenation or rest and might give rise to burnouts that affect other areas of life negatively.

Qualified men with ADHD who are prepared to define the duration of their hyper-focus sessions and insert breaks between them achieve a greater sense of welfare and better work-life balance.

- **Balancing Passion with Practicality**

While passion is influential, it is also important to have a balanced perspective and not overlook the fact of financial stability or long-term goals. The magical side of identifying love and practicality simultaneously will lead to one's improvement and fulfillment.

Risk Management and Decision Making

Instantly, the sign of ADHD, which is impulsivity, may lead to improper impulses and risky decisions. However, by developing effective risk management strategies, adult men with ADHD can harness their spontaneity while mitigating potential negative consequences.

- **Impulsivity Controls and Risk Assessment**

Learning to pause before acting on impulses and assessing potential risks can be a valuable skill for individuals with ADHD. Techniques, such as mindfulness practices, cognitive-behavioral therapy (CBT), and seeking input from trusted advisors can help cultivate a more balanced approach to decision-making.

- **Seeking Feedback and Second Opinions**

While impulsivity can lead to quick decisions, it's essential to balance this trait with input from others. Seeking feedback and second opinions from trusted friends, family members, or professionals can provide valuable perspectives and help mitigate potential risks.

Also adult men with ADHD who regularly sought feedback from their support networks reported making more informed decisions and experiencing fewer negative consequences from impulsive actions.

- **Learning from Mistakes and Failures**

Embracing failures and learning from mistakes is a crucial aspect of personal growth. Individuals with ADHD may face more frequent setbacks due to impulsivity or inattention, but these experiences can serve as valuable learning opportunities if approached with a growth mindset.

Creative and Strategic Thinking

Many individuals with ADHD possess remarkable creativity and the ability to approach problems from unique angles, which can be invaluable assets in various aspects of life.

- **Embracing Divergent Thinking**

Divergent thinking, or the ability to generate novel and unconventional ideas, is a strength often associated with ADHD. By embracing this trait, adult men with ADHD can foster creativity, innovation, and find innovative solutions to challenges.

- **Problem Solving in Unique Ways**

Individuals with ADHD often possess the ability to see patterns and connections that others may overlook, leading to unique problem-solving approaches. By leveraging this strength, adult men with ADHD can tackle complex challenges and find innovative solutions.

Adult men with ADHD who were tutored to be proud of their particular manner of solving problems were in a higher position on the scales of creativity, job satisfaction, and overall life satisfaction than those who were taught to subdue their characteristic problem-solving approach.

- **Seeing Opportunities in Challenges**

ADHD may ingrain that mind, which sees barriers as a door opening for self-improvement and refreshing solutions to problems. Using the tools of rethinking and replacing hurdles with new angles and solutions, a man with ADHD can develop a state of being increasingly resilient and developing himself.

Personal Goals and Motivation

Formulation and resolution of self-directed objectives provide personal development. This allows individuals to concentrate on their core strengths and overcome difficult obstacles with the help of practical target-setting and the mobilization of intrinsic motivation.

- **Setting SMART Goals**

The (Specific, Measurable, Achievable, Relevant, and Time-bound) goal-setting model provides an invaluable setting for ADHD individuals to achieve their goals. Through cutting the broad aims into exact and definite stages, it ensures they concentrate on the matter at hand and mark their success.

- **Creating Accountability Systems**

Transparency systems, such as communicating with your closest friend or family member, grouping together for a support session, or even using a productivity app, are very useful in staying on track with your goals.

Also it was seen that adult men with ADHD who sought diligence mechanisms used to be more successful than ADHD people without accountability systems.

- **Finding Intrinsic Motivation**

While the choice of external stimulators such as awards or recognition might be persuasive, unlocking the intrinsic motivation, which is the spontaneous driving force, could be extremely powerful and especially useful for adults with

ADHD. Through connecting their goals with their values, interests, and passions, adults with ADHD can develop a whole-hearted attitude towards life, and such a base would fuel their internal drive.

Inspirational Success Stories

Though thinking about ADHD as a curse is natural, the fact that there are real-life inspirational stories about adult men who have channeled their strengths to surmount the hurdles they encounter and do amazing things can be encouraging.

Influential people and achievers, such as successful business leaders and top athletes, are some people who have excelled in the challenges of ADHD. Learning their life stories can be an inspiration to us, and the knowledge we can gain from their challenges and successes can help us realize our strengths and our ability to move past hurdles.

Thus, to take a specific example, Richard Branson, who is the founder of the Virgin Group, has been quite open about his ADHD and believes that he has made his name because of his capability to think outside the box and to assess certain risks. (Book: An approach psychology by farkhandjha shahnaaz)

- **Overcoming Adversity**

Many of the famous individuals who had ADHD have had to fight many fights in their lives, from personal battles to social prejudice or professional obstacles. Through their narratives about coping and endurance, their experiences could really teach people what to aim for with the help of ambition and a positive attitude.

- **Finding Purpose and Fulfillment**

Besides the outer success, so many people living with ADHD have now discovered virtue and fulfillment through fully accepting their rare qualities, as well as utilizing them to make the world better. Their stories will certainly be an uplifting factor for individuals and can eventually help in their own life to find meaning and satisfaction.

One of the most compelling narratives is that of Adam Levine, the frontman for Maroon 5 and "The Voice" coach who was diagnosed with ADHD during his youth. Through exhausting his limitless creative energy, he has become a widely known singer and mentor, which has certainly motivated many fans.

These stories, therefore, act as a personification of the fact that ADHD may be looked at as an ability rather than a limitation. It is a distinctive set of strengths that one can use as a source of invention, development, and make a positive impact on the world.

Finally, ADHD can be a source of both challenges and growth. Unlike other people, ADHD can be used as a positive trait, and individuals can lead successful lives and professional careers by concentrating deeply on the condition, being creative, and solving problems. With an open mind and supportive individuals, adult men diagnosed with ADHD can turn their situation into an opportunity to become a better person at a higher level.

Chapter 7

The path of a man with ADHD as an adult is hardly easy, and a support system that can stand on its own can ease the journey. This section focuses on different ways to create a powerful and wide support system, such as finding friends on campus, getting professional help, collaborating with community resources, and promoting family support. Developing a viable support system for males living with ADHD can be vital with the resources, expertise, and reassurance they can gain.

Identifying Allies

The first thing is to make a plan for the kind of climate that can provide you with friends and mentors. These allies might provide emotional support and give some advice; they may become a place to vent and help us out during difficult periods.

- **Family Members and Friends**

However, there is another category of human factors, which are your loving family members and close friends, that can help you overcome the problem. Through their brave revelation of ADHD and educating their family and friends on this condition, adult men become a source of wisdom, and they find strength within their networks. However, it is important to keep in mind that these conversations must be conducted skillfully, as some family members and friends can easily be surprised by the complexities of ADHD.

- **Support Groups and Peer Networks**

Interacting with others who have a life story like yours can be extremely beneficial to provide a supportive environment and understanding. Within this space, people can share their problems and triumphs, as well as get access to hands-on, instructive information that will help to manage not only emotional stress but also the stress that can occur during the healing process. These groups can either be with the help of local organizations or mental health professionals; online platforms can help us find other people who suffer from similar issues.

- **Mental Health Professionals**

Psychologists specializing in ADHD may offer the know-how, validated methods, and empathetic view that may better enable male adults with ADHD to master the complexities of living with the disorder.

Professional Help

Although social support groups are now seen as something necessary to manage ADHD, experts in qualified fields can really improve a person's ability to control their symptoms and improve their well-being.

- **Therapy and Counseling Options:**

Cognitive-behavioral therapy (CBT), mindfulness-based therapies, and other forms of counseling have been shown to greatly benefit adult males with ADHD. These treatments can be the foundation for individuals to deal with whatever life throws at them, improve their self-control over their emotions, and help patients with other mental health problems like anxiety or depression.

Also adult men with ADHD who had CBT reported that, at the end of the program, they had notable improvements in managing impulsivity, enhancing focus and concentration, and developing healthy coping mechanisms.

- **ADHD Coaching Services**

Individuals with ADHD sometimes need specialized trainers known as ADHD coaches, who provide customized management strategies and guidance for managing the condition. These mentors can assist men with the ability to have advanced organizational skills, learn the best time management techniques, and have goal-setting strategies tailored for them.

- **Medication Management**

Taking into consideration that many people with ADHD take medication as one aspect of a multi-faceted approach to treatment, overall, medication management involves working closely with physicians, i.e., psychiatrists or psychiatric nurse practitioners, who ensure that the proper dosage is administered, side effects are monitored, and the efficacy of the prescribed medication is constantly assessed.

Community Resources

Members of family, friends, and industry experts with extensive experience can offer meaningful support both in terms of information and social interaction.

- **Online Forums and Communities**

The internet has provided people with ADHD with a mass specter of online platforms that include groups, social media, and virtual communities, with the main purpose of supporting these individuals. These platforms become a place for communicating for those who may want to talk about their lives and experiences, get recommendations, and meet up with people who have gone through the same experiences.

- **Local Support Groups and Workshops**

The very thing that many communities are providing are actual in-person support groups, along with more specific educational workshops for individuals with ADHD and their loved ones. These events serve as the perfect ground for the physical exchange of knowledge and interacting with experts. They also create a favorable environment for individuals to relate to each other, who may be on similar journeys.

- **Educational Seminars and Webinars**

Becoming knowledgeable about the ongoing studies, ADHD management techniques, and treatment approaches can be transformational. Attending educational seminars, listening to workshops, or attending webinars held by respectable organizations or health professionals at a high capacity can leave adult men with the knowledge they need to make the right decision in their treatment.

Family Dynamics

While ADHD is typically viewed as an individual disease state, it in truth offers far-reaching effects on family relationships and dynamics. To build up a sustainable support system is to imply creating understanding and collaboration within the family.

- **Educating Loved Ones about ADHD**

The greatest difficulty faced by men with ADHD aged 18+ might be the absence of knowledge and peer support from their loved ones. Through keeping family members informed about the hardships of ADHD, the symptoms, and how they directly affect the individual, people can raise human interest and create a supportive environment that touches everyone.

A finding that members of the households who participated in ADHD psychoeducation psychology department gcuf h workshops mentioned receiving more support, becoming more empathetic, and also learning how to work together more effectively to solve ADHD-related problems was noted.

- **Establishing Supportive Relationships**

Parents and children in a family must be open to communicating with each other. One thing they must do is have patience. Parents must develop this skill, but they must always understand their children. Men with ADHD in their adulthood should be able to describe their particular obstacles and needs; however, they should somewhat share and consider the issues and experiences of their partners or family members.

- **Collaborative Problem-Solving**

Rather than viewing ADHD's related challenges as individual concerns only, the more effective way to overcome them is by involving the whole family in the process of joint problem-solving, which can help establish a feeling of belonging to one team and having common interests. Utilizing a collective approach to find solutions that are grounded in reality, people living with ADHD and their families can instead put in place a support system that assists individuals to develop and grow into healthier people.

In conclusion, having a supportive environment is the fundamental factor that should be part of handling ADHD in adult men. Through the identification of support groups, talking with professionals, utilizing other available support services within the community, and the practice of having a nurturing family environment, each person can ultimately collect enough support that will allow them to surpass the hurdles of ADHD with strength and dedication. It is essential to know that you are not alone on this trip, and so as long as you trust and get the help of the available people, you will unveil your fullness and live a great life.

CONCLUSION

ADHD is an endless voyage of self-discovery and self-determination. Knowing the neurological dynamics and carefully developing specific skills could allow you to transform disadvantages into strengths. Use the knowledge that you garnered by designing an actionable plan that will suit you and your specific needs in the fields of work, relationships, and personal development. Along with embracing ADHD as a lifelong process, refine the coping methods as the situation develops. Celebrate all your successes, reflect on the areas for improvement, and lean on your support network. Through commitment and perseverance, you can leverage your neurodiverse mind to flourish in a way that best suits you.

THANK YOU

Just wanted to let you know how much you mean to me.

Without your help and attention, I couldn't keep making helpful publications like this one.

Once again, I appreciate you reading this book. I absolutely enjoyed writing it, and I hope you did too.

Before you leave, I need you to do me a favor.

Please consider posting a book review for this one on the platform.

Reviews will be used to help my writing.

Your feedback is extremely helpful to me and will help me to generate more. upcoming books in the information genre.

I would love to hear from you.

Dori Natasha Gentlekins.

References

Attention Deficit Disorder Association. (n.d.). ADHD Symptoms in Men.

Mayo Clinic Staff. (n.d.). Adult ADHD. Mayo Clinic.

Tietjen, L. (n.d.). Adult ADHD: Symptoms, Statistics, Causes, Diagnosis, and Treatment. Healthline.

Choosing Therapy. (n.d.). ADHD in Men: Symptoms, Causes, and Treatment.

Dodson, W. (n.d.). How ADHD Ignites Rejection Sensitive Dysphoria in Men. ADDitude.

ADHD Centre. (n.d.). ADHD for Men.

NeuroHealth Associates. (n.d.). ADHD in Adult Men.

Smith, J. (n.d.). Is ADHD More Common in Males or Females? Medical News Today.

ADHD Centre. (n.d.). Female vs Male ADHD.

ShiftGrit. (n.d.). What Is It Like to Have ADHD in Men?

DSM-5

Printed by Libri Plureos GmbH in Hamburg,
Germany